# Ten Seasons

# Ten Seasons

explorations in Botanics
edited by Gerry Loose
photographs by Morven Gregor

SCOTTISH POETRY LIBRARY

By leaves we live

in association with Luath Press Limited

First published in 2007 by
Scottish Poetry Library
5 Crichton's Close
Canongate
Edinburgh EH8 8DT

Luath Press Ltd
54 3/2 Castlehill
The Royal Mile
Edinburgh EH1 2ND

ISBN: 978 1905222 80 3
ISBN: 1 905222 80 7

The publishers gratefully acknowledge the support of the
Scottish Arts Council and Glasgow City Council  towards the
publication of this volume.

Designed by Barrie Tullett
Typeset in Enigma and Printed on Omnia
Printed and bound in Lincolnshire by Wayzgoose

## CONTENTS

words at the bottom of pages were those brought or sent for a May Day celebration

## IN MEMORIAM GAEL TURNBULL
## 1928-2004

My thanks to all the gardeners and writers, singers, musicians, artists & performers without whose help & enthusiasm none of this could have happened.

In addition to those mentioned by name in the book, thanks to

Ewen Donaldson, Paul Matthews, Louise Bustard, John Logan, David Menzies, Martin O'Loughlin, Lynsey Boyd, Steven Jakusz, Iain Traynor and all staff at the Botanic Gardens, Glasgow: I cannot thank them enough for their helpfulness, courtesy, advice & assistance.

Jenny Brown; Gavin Wallace of the Scottish Arts Council; Catherine McInerney, Councillor Stevenson, Councillor Alex Mosson of Glasgow City Council; Linda Grey, Mary Gibson & pupils from East Park School; Tomiko Shirakata (Mizumura), Masami Arao, Hiroshi Ota, Mandors Textiles, Grassroots Café, Marlborough Marble & Stone Works, Loxley Colour, Quigg's of Glasgow, From Buds to Petals, Friends of the Glasgow Botanic Gardens, Nobuo Kanematsu of the Kyoto Botanical Garden, Hortus Botanicus Amsterdam, John Ainslie & Jane Tallents of Scottish CND; Rena McEwan, Jim McGlashan, Hilary Nicoll, Jim McGurrin & Robert Stewart of the Botanic Writers' Group; Grace Kitengi, Behzad Karimi, Omer Ali Artan, Ali Yagliyurt, Seri Selvakumar, Gajan Kamalanathan, Arnaud Touanga, Marjaneh Tajik, Dmitry Fescenko, Nawras Mahmood, Elspeth Brown, Kenneth C Steven, Gösta Ågren, Arne Ruste, Hester Hedges, Houra Qadir, Adil Ibrahim, Yama Yari, Allan Tall, Anne Chaurand, Tommy Smith, Davy Crichton, Gillian Frame, Findlay Napier, Tom Richardson, Fionn MacArthur, AL Kennedy, EK Reeder, Drew Campbell, Donald Beveridge, Chris Dolan, Simon McKerrell, Dave Wilde, Lana McLachlan, Larry Butler, Donny O'Rourke, Anne Thomson, Sally Evans, the late George Bruce, Val Forsyth, Allison Galbraith, Nancy Clunas,

Robyn Marsack, Jim C Wilson, Robin Bell, Tom Bryan, Ingrid Lees, David Bellingham, Tom Hubbard, Sandy Hutchison, Tessa Ransford, Robin Lloyd-Jones, David Mellin, Laini Chrismas, Brian Hartley, Isa Luque, Angela Blacklock-Brown, Anne MacLeod, Graham Hartill; & all those from the Dominican Republic, Spain & California, who sent or brought words & poems to the Botanics. May Sarton, 'A Glass of Water', *Collected Poems 1930-1993* (W.W.Norton & Co. Inc, 1993), by permission of A.M. Heath & Co. Ltd.

*If there are people whose names I have accidentally left out, please accept my apologies & my thanks to you too.*

### Acknowledgements

The editor and publishers thank the poets for their generous permission to print/ reprint copyright poems, and acknowledge the appearance of some of them in other publications:

Meg Bateman, 'Kiss', *Fred Beake/Nicholas Moore/Meg Bateman Etruscan reader IX* (Etruscan Books, 2000); Ron Butlin, 'Absinthe with Eddie', *Without a Backward Glance: new and selected poems* (Barzan, 2006); Gerry Cambridge, 'The Sundew's Speech, *'Nothing but heather!': Scottish nature in poems, photographs and prose* (Luath Press, 1999); Stewart Conn, 'In the Kibble Palace', *In the Kibble Palace: poems new and* selected (Bloodaxe, 1987); Anna Crowe, 'Scops Owl', *Punk with Dulcimer* (Peterloo, 2006); Kathleen Jamie, 'Meadowsweet', *Jizzen* (Picador, 1999); Tom Leonard, 'The Underfunder's Utopia', 'Walking in the Park', *access to the silence* (Etruscan Books, 2004); Liz Lochhead, 'The Beekeeper', *The Colour of Black and White* (Polygon, 2003); Peter Manson, 'Lithops divergens', *For the Good of* Liars (Barque Press, 2006); Don McKay, 'The Song for the Song of the White-Throated Sparrow', *Another Gravity* (McClelland & Stewart Inc., 2000); Edwin Morgan, 'At Eighty', *Unknown Is Best* (Mariscat/Scottish Poetry Library, 2000); Liz Niven, *Cree Lines* (Dumfries & Galloway Arts Association, 2000); Vikram Seth, 'All you who sleep tonight', *All You Who Sleep Tonight* (Faber & Faber, 1990); Maud Sulter, 'West', *Zabat: poetics of a family tree* (Urban Fox Pres, 1989); Gael Turnbull, 'Wandering onto a beach', 'A Perception of Ferns', *There are words*; *Collected Poems* (Shearsman Books/Mariscat, 2006); Kenneth White, from *House of Tides*, *Letters from Brittany and other lands of the West* (Polygon, 2000), pp.61-2; Jan Zwicky, from 'Kant and Bruckner', *Songs for Relinquishing the Earth* (Brick Books, 1998).

# INTRODUCTION

Plants and poems share a common rootstock, not only in grammar, but in the jubilation of their wild, wayward growth, abundance of grace and form and the nourishment they provide.

The Japanese poet Matsuo Bashō, on hearing women sing a planting song in the rice paddies wrote

the beginning of culture!

a rice planting song

in the heartland

which caused one commentator to ask: 'Isn't a rice planting song the spontaneous voice of the soil?'

The fact that plants we grow for nourishment may also be beautiful (and therefore cultivated beyond economic need) is a phenomenon that constantly delights. That the human outpourings of grief and love, hope and despair that we call poetry have a wild beauty is no surprise. That *wildness* is at the heart of it all. Without it there is no wealth: we do not create plants, only gardens.

Paradoxically we work to keep wildness at bay in our gardens. Any garden is a staking out of boundaries from the surrounding land and preventing incursion from those unwanted plants which have become weeds.

Increasingly, gardeners are threatened also by wildness of a peculiarly human kind – the wilful blindness of planners and developers – who see no profit from agriculture or horticulture and certainly none from poetry, and who would cut off the one source of wealth we have on the planet.

Fortunately there are oases in all this, and maybe the cycle of exploitation of land is again approaching a more symbiotic phase as we realise that without wildness there is nothing from which we can draw our own livelihood and plant the seeds and celebrate the harvests with song, which we may pass to the next generation.

One such oasis is the Botanic Garden in Glasgow. Much loved, it is a model of a garden – not just admired, but used by the people of Glasgow. Here on any given day are children playing, with another generation sitting on benches; courting takes place in the hot houses and among the shady trees; on those self same benches are memorial plaques to people now dead but whose absent presence remains strong. Here may be heard a dozen or more languages as spoken by citizens taking simple pleasure in that carefully- (indeed, lovingly-) tended wildness of a great Botanic Garden.

It was to this Garden I was appointed Poet in Residence, first by the Poetry Society for six months, then by Glasgow City Council (Councillors of which agreed that a garden has more than one season to celebrate). And from the beginning, I saw my job as a celebration. Celebrating the remarkable skill, resourcefulness and versatility of those who cultivate both usefulness and beauty for the rest of us to enjoy; celebrating those who labour at the real true edge of culture. And with them, the fruits of their labour: the plants and thus, poetry.

My tenure at the Botanics, as it is known to all and sundry, became a three-year celebration during which in some small ways I was able to help restore a little of the culture of poetry to its rightful place.

That this touched the lives of thousands of people in Glasgow and the wider world is testament to the need for not just culture (I use the word in its original sense), but the cultivation of an inner wildness, unpredictability and spontaneity which we celebrate with poetry. As anyone who has ever planted a seed and seen its germination knows, there can be no greater wonder – it fills the heart with a wild exhilaration, which has its natural culmination in poetry and song.

Of course in all this I was welcomed by Botanic staff, then willingly aided and abetted by scores of poets as well as gardeners (who were often both together). City councillors also saw other benefits of attracting more people to use the Garden; we reached out also to the world of commerce – our endeavours were often underwritten by the generous sponsorship of local businesses – from the wine we drank at our events (not just the heady intoxication of plants and poems!) to the ribbons on which were written poems to hang in trees. The media also had a great deal of fun in all this, with easy copy and fine stories of people enjoying themselves in an old way that crosses boundaries and cultures in the shared pleasure of mingling to common purpose in a garden.

What you hold in your hands is a curious hybrid: not simply a book of poetry, nor a record of plants, nor yet of poets among plants (and there were so many who over the course of three years came to express themselves in poetry); rather like a plant in which the wild ancestor is apparent and enjoyed for its own sake as much as the usefulness of its offspring with which it shares genetic material. A hybrid which was born out of necessity; the necessity to cultivate and celebrate. This book is a record, certainly not a how-to manual; but if it enthuses and allows others to cultivate their own gardens, if it introduces a new audience to gardens and to poetry and ways in which they may *usefully* be combined, then it will have succeeded as much as the three years of seed sowing at Glasgow Botanics which I shared with many others, most of them far more experienced cultivators (and celebrators!) than me.

*Gerry Loose*

# Events

Some of the events scheduled have yet to take place. Some are still taking place as you read this, acted out by natural phenomena:

Saturday March 7 1998 published (on the internet) at 18:54 GMT UK
Earthquake on Scottish West Coast: An earthquake has shaken residents in the west of Scotland but no damage or injuries have been reported.
The British Geological Survey (BGS) said the tremor measured 2.7 on the Richter Scale. Glenn Ford, a seismologist at the BGS Edinburgh, described the earthquake as significant. (See item 3 below.)

Everything made use of; everything adapted to our need.
Please feel free to stage any event from the list here. There is no copyright to imagination.

dew event

birdsong event

earth tremor
introduction to earthquakes

meteor showers
quadrantid meteor showers
comet storms
(consult your local astronomer)

*from the Dominican Republic, each word on a cloth banner:*    chicorita    amor plant poems

label dreams

snow viewing

moon viewing

multilingual namings

theoretical namings
by scent
by texture
by taste

This cloud does change
with the movements
of the moon and the
narrow the quite
narrow suggestion of
the building.

candle floating

gardening the sky

steam event

It does and then when
it is settled and no
sounds differ then
comes the moment
when cheerfulness is so
assured that there is an
occasion.

season ticket

snow collection permit

leaf collection permit

wind assessors permit

capturing twilight

leaf counting event

cloud naming event

stolen fruits

earth tracing

following bees

assisting spiders

Full Moon ○
Last Quarter ☽
New Moon ●
First Quarter ☾

Gertrude Stein
from the invitation to
*MOON WALK an occasion*
at the Botanic Gardens
on the night of the full
moon 6th June 2001 with
Professor John Brown
Astronomer Royal for
Scotland. Full-moon tea
was served

respeto   felicidad   rebeldia

# Permissions & Bulletins

## OFFICE OF THE POET
## IN RESIDENCE

### AUTUMN LEAF COLLECTION PERMIT

This permit is issued to


who is in full possession of all permissions required to collect fallen leaves from any species of tree in any quantity within the perimeter of the Botanic Gardens for the purposes of poetic or artistic endeavour, political agitation or the lobbying of governments or their agents.

**It is to be noted** that the permit is free and may not be sold or exchanged for goods or services. It is, however, transferable. The licence holder is **not permitted** to assist the early fall of said leaves, nor to effect removal from the tree by any means mechanical or by the means of stone-throwing or stick-hurling or the launching of any other missile, whether by natural or mechanical means. [Such extraction is the subject of a *Standing Tree-Leaf Order*, issued by the *Office of the Curator*, and is issued only in respect of a particular species, not to exceed the extraction of more than five (5) leaves per species per season.]

## OFFICE OF THE POET
## IN RESIDENCE

Department of Mountains & Waters
**ONE DAY DREAMING PERMIT**

This permit is issued to

who may dream all day, on any selected
single day in the year of issue.
Length of day to be determined by permit holder,
according to local conditions.

Valid in any hemisphere.

**PLEASE NOTE**:
Under certain circumstances, dreams
(***but not Permit***) may be transferable.
**SEE OVERLEAF**

paciencia    amistad    la umanidad

**OFFICE OF THE POET
IN RESIDENCE**

BULLETIN No. 1

This office is seeking

**ASSESSORS OF BREEZES & GALES
(W & SW quadrants)**

Duties: to issue sporadic reports
on all aspects of air movement.
(See below for suggested format)

Interested parties may contact

BOTANIC GARDENS
730 Great Western Road
Glasgow G12 0UE

*(sample report format)*

Fair. Good. Warnings of gales.
Consider transparency, fog & the flight of herons
the spring & fall of riffled water
the dying of breath & the steam of speech in winter
the curve, wave & roll of hurricanes.
Small songs are escaping to quieter galaxies.
Love is making the air lucid
SW backing SE.

[One appointment was made, from the person whose
application impressed the most]:

Application for position of
Assessor of Breezes & Gales
from M G
with consultant advice from Kokopelli.

The prospective assessors envisage
capturing on film evidence of breezes and
gales at work and play,
developing the feather scale of wind
measurement,
issuing quotations from various sources on
the movement of air, and most importantly,
talking to and toasting winds of all directions.

hermandad    comunicación    el compañerismo

# The Valentine Tree

When I first discovered that there are remains of St Valentine in Glasgow, at that time stored in a dusty cardboard box in Blessed John Duns Scotus in the Gorbals (now in a new casket in St Francis' Church), I knew this was something to be pursued.

It has long been a tradition in Scotland, as elsewhere in the world, to tie ribbons and cloths to trees (hence the Scots *clootie* tree) associated with healing wells and places of pilgrimage as votive offerings: prayers and wishes and thanks. This tradition has something of the same urge as the preservation of remains and relics, and it seemed only fitting to blow off some dust and welcome St Valentine back by tying poems of love in a tree in the Botanics on his day – February 14th.

That first year invitations went out via word of mouth, letter, newspaper, radio and TV stories for people to send in a poem to be tied to the huge fern-leaved beech tree at the main gates to the Botanic Gardens. By the 14th, hundreds had arrived; Scotland being Scotland in February, they had to be tied to the tree in a blizzard from the top of a ladder. Of course people were also invited to tie their own poem at noon and after, which hundreds more did, since the sun had by then made an appearance.

The day continued with poets reading in the Kibble Palace, the enormous rectilinear cast-iron glasshouse in the Botanics, and with musicians. Also, Gar-Ming Hui demonstrated the art of Chinese paper-folding, showing how to fold winged hearts and doves, which many folk then spontaneously wrote on and hung in the Valentine Tree. The event continued until dusk that day. Latecomers continued tying poems all week.

The Valentine Tree continued to grow, subsequent years seeing the same type of event, but with ever-increasing numbers of poems tied to the tree. Most poems were washed away by rain and bleached by sun; some remain.

That first invitation contained these lines of Robert Burns, himself not unknown to love:

Wi' plenty o' sic trees, I trow
The world would live in peace

The slight hearing loss
we each suffer from
means we sometimes
fail to catch the sense
of ends of sentences
but what we do not fail
to grasp and gasp at are the
vertiginous moments
of all this passion stuff –
like the fat magpie
balancing on the phone wire
outside the window:
of course it's going to fall
and of course it doesn't.

Hamish Whyte

under the clear moon

two birds flying west

with a single flute

Kevin MacNeil
handwritten & sent on a
white ribbon

## To a horse, fallen on the ice and weeping

Oh, horse, you needn't.
Horse, listen,
Which of us can think
      ourselves better than you?
Little one,
All of us have something of
      the horse in us.
Every one of us shares
      Your horse-nature

Mayakovsky
translated by Alison
Prince & sent by her
in the original written
on a 100 rouble note
with translation on the
other side.

*from Scotland:*   amadeus   resonance

**Amorous Greetings**
*in terms of glass*

### (1) its origins

If the first glass was not planned
in advance but just happened
by the correct ingredients
coming together in the right circumstances

then it was much as it was for us
and only needed recognition
and appreciation of what was possible
and wonder at the result.

Jill Turnbull
pasted on a wide blue
ribbon tied with a
narrow white ribbon.

### (2) its shaping

Not for me at first sight
or second or any such
stuttering progression

but as a gather of glass
may expand into completion –
not moulded or pressed or cut

but unconstrained
and finding its own shape
from within – thus literally

## Our Day

Gales –
        force five
driving rain in
        the face
and sleet
and sun
        breaking through
for
a second only.
Enough,
for you to come
to me.

Michael
handwritten on a
Glasgow Botanic
Gardens postcard

*from Wales*:   nincompoop   chthonic   faster

**Kiss**

Our first kiss, a kiss of parting,
And all night my mind rocked
By the warmth of your lips,
My heart again filled with a useless longing,
The Minch and twenty years between us,
As I try to turn my mind to tidying up the toys,
Try to turn my regard
Into the regard of a mother.

Meg Bateman
on a heart shaped piece
of paper

# Love

A friend told me
That another friend sends her love

All the way from New Orleans
But that it'll be

Maybe another five weeks
Before it actually arrives

Rody Gorman

*in Scots:* clanjamphrie    dreich

## Scops Owl
*for Julian*

At night I lie without you
under a pelt of darkness
heavy with cypress
ragged with goat-cries.

Under the white moon's Roman coin
dogs are barking from distant farms
with little rips of sound
that stone walls catch, throw back.

All this he draws like silk
through a gold ring
into a single woodwind note:
a true and level fluting,

Anna Crowe

tongued and sweet,
I picture travelling
through night's horizons
north, to where you sleep.

## The Bowl of Beads

Who would not
love my wife's
        beads?
A pink bowlful,
gathered not
out of industry
or perseverance,
but out of luck
& the love of
        her eye.
Whatever's
been unstrung,
whatever's
fallen from
        the crust
that held it,
slipped between
your fingers –
        a brightness
suddenly lost
in the dull, work-
        a day world –
you've no need
to regret it:
my wife's
taken it
as serendipitous
treasure to add
to her cornu-
        copia

of light, her
        collective
sigh of colour.
Who would not
love my wife's
        beads?
If you were
my young
        daughter,
would you not
run your
        small hands
through the cool-
ness of them
run them
like water,
the light
        behind them,
through your
        small fists.
I know you would
& bear them
        before you –
the brimful
        of them –
as does she
small smiling
        priestess
across a carpet
of scattered toys.

waefu' scunner

What I cannot
        tell –
because of my
        own confusion
is how you'd feel,
if you were she
& saw such a
rich bowl tip
from your hands
        those beads
waterfalling
into space –
        never
had there seemed so many,
never had they
        seemed
so bright,
        the thick
galaxy of them,
the arcing
rainbow of them,
stotting on the
        carpet
like hailstones.
        But
        sorry, no, no
        sorry –
        let this be
        what they were
        always for – a

cascading
        spending
a fluid
        giving;
as sometimes
        stalled,
we may see
        our love
before us,
        as colour,
movement
        and light –
before it gathers
to our shape again
        we hold it
        as will
once more this bowl
these beads.

Tom Pow
handwritten on a long
strip of white card
fastened with white
ribbon

she is the white wave blown by the wind

she is the wind that blows the white wave

Hamish Whyte
on a white ribbon

*from the Ehama people at Santa Cruz:*   cogitate   sumptuous

## Ghazal

The shutter opens
a warm wind sifts the room.

We look down at the uneven ground,
see the tender life by the stream.

Sip dew from new hawthorn leaves,
taste the river as you swim out.

The smell of love
is honey in the right place.

Your voice deep in my heart,
we sing our song, together.

Jayne Wilding

## Meadowsweet

*Tradition suggests that certain of the Gaelic*
*women poets were buried face down.*


So they buried her, and turned home,
a drab psalm
hanging about them like haar,

not knowing the liquid
trickling from her lips
would seek its way down,

and that caught in her slowly
unravelling plait of grey hair
were summer seeds:

meadowsweet, bastard balm,
tokens of honesty, already
beginning their crawl

toward light, so showing her,
when the time came,
how to dig herself out –

to surface and greet them,
mouth young, and full again
of dirt, and spit, and poetry.

Kathleen Jamie
at the celebration of
the 2000 Valentine Tree

re-membering    abundance    saratoga

**West**

Generations

Coming home was not
a visit to my
father's compound
but some hours spent
in dialogue with you.

Africa waits patiently you said
She will always be here.

Your

    limbs

        so

           beautiful

Maud Sulter
at the celebration of the    I fear not touch
2002 Valentine Tree

        for fear
        of becoming
        addicted
        to such
        perfection.

**Touch and Go**
*The study of socio-sexual dynamics of single parenthood, in*
*Glasgow's Botanics*


Reveals a familiar scenario
The syndrome o the touch an go Lothario
A wiltin wallflooer draps its heid, ill-fated
That some B.'s one night stand, has impregnated

Sheena Blackhall
at the celebration of
the 2000 Valentine Tree
when she also sang
Burns' songs

*also from Scotland:*    haecceitas    bakea

## Planted Poems

Poems were 'planted' on labels and notices next to the plants they concern, in the glasshouses and outside. Like the plants, they formed an ephemeral display, and were removed when the plant had seen its annual cycle through.

It was also fun to arrange standard botanic labels in odd corners where wild plants had made their incursions.

## Lithops divergens

no returned breath

by day the half-heart

lord of its own

supply                changes self

for self

smaller than poem

& giving nothing away

Peter Manson

felix   satori   l'huard

# The Sundew's Speech

I skinkle here and wait
to be the insect's fate.
Admire if you will how light
turns my kind to a bright
galaxy of ruby and of green,
though it's not beauty that I mean
but the marriage of function and need.
Come, prey, let your clambering greed
find its end in my pinpoint glues –
I'll enfold you like a lover, use
your body's life, open and let
the wind blow your husk away, then set
in place again each fatal coronet.

Gerry Cambridge

gypsophila   МИР   solīdařtāt

## Anemone nemorosa

Among the first to fumble
in the waking of spring,
the wood anemones'
pink-flushed white stars
come out to twinkle
before the beech leaves
send them back to sleep.

Colin Will

## Galanthus nivalis

March is my most active period.
In May and June
my sessions – 30,000 guineas a shot – carry on
and officially come to a climax in July
when I go and enjoy
the freedom of the paddocks all day.

Up to November I'm dead as a rule
but then, round about Christmas-tide,
foreplanning gets underway
for the coming season!

The 1st of January
my own birthday, as you may be aware
is the official birthday of every thoroughbred
and you, meantime, are probably maiden
or perhaps even more frisky than usual
after last year's covering – remember?

Hang on in there,
my little
filly, my little snowdrop! Never fear!
After Monday 14th February,
ie St Valentine's Day,
it's official:
the mare(s) may be jumped by the stallion again!

Rody Gorman

kucing    pangur    braggadocio

# Meuran-na-mnatha-sidhe

Seilleanan trang a' siubhal
meuranan na mnatha-sìdhe:
is cinnteach nach eil na tha sin
de mheuran oirre, is meuran air gach aon,
no a bheil an leas làn de mhnathan-sìdhe?
Dh'fheumadh tu coimputair fìor làidir
gu cùnntadh na tha sin de mhnathan-sidhe
air feadh na dùthcha,
's gach tè trang le snàthad is snàithlean
a' cumail an t-saoghail an òrdugh,
ach dhan t-seillean
chan eil an sin ach faoineas,
tha a choimpiutair fhèin aig'
's a shaoghal air a riaghladh
eadar sgeap is meuran
gus an tuit iad uile gu talamh.

Derick Thomson

mitość   ishq   grasyas

Reynoutria japonica (Houtt.)

JAPANESE KNOTWEED

*The most appalling thug.*

---

Rumex obtusifolius (L.)

DOCKEN

*An offender.*

Gerry Loose
labels for unwanted
plants

## The Pond

All good gardeners make use of available resources. In the Kibble Palace at Glasgow Botanic Gardens is a round pond in which koi carp in all their colours chase their fishy dreams. Its reflective surface made an ideal spot to take visitors unaware and open possibilities of poetry. At the time the pond contained an island on which was a venerable specimen of Royal Fern.

I wanted an imaginative use of the pond, and asked the late Gael Turnbull to make something there (as well as a poet of quiet excellence and great influence, he was a maker of poetry machines, which intrigue and excite in their innovative ways of presenting poems). What Gael made was typical of his erudition and modesty and his attention to detail: it exceeded expectation and delighted all who saw it.

His circular poem with no end or beginning was simple and effective in making use of the water and the presence of the Royal Fern. The poem here has an arbitrary 'first' line and is one-dimensional, the original having been made in mirror writing and hung round the pond in such a way as only to be read in the surface of the water, with reflected sky and the delicate tracings of the Kibble's smaller dome adding a further dimension to the words. It was both an echo of and echoed the carp swimming round in a dream circle: in my end is my beginning.

It stayed in place by public demand for many months.

diffusing ferns

with fronds unfolding

for the eye to reach

mirrored beneath

inverted searchings

of wavering croziers

to find reflection

by reflecting on

as shadowed light

so spores are shed

dispersions made

from unseen source

conceived to generate

flowering invisibly

made manifest

freshly apparent

by shoots asserting

what was concealed

and here reflected

Gael Turnbull

coìmhearsnachd   yaa'aat'eeh   kun

## Inscription For The Manor Pool

Singing
you dropped me in the silver.

I wish I was the wisest fish,
the golden-age's bubble-talker,
*carpe diem*, the fish of laughter.

I wish I was the privilege fish,
the gold who waits within the water –
who sees, who feels,
who knows the bathing daughter.

Richard Price
poem hung round the
pond at the launch of
his book *Renfrewshire in
Old Photographs*
(with Raymond Friel,
Mariscat 2000)

## The Botanical Basho

The Botanical Basho is a small book (published during this period by the *ad hoc* Botanics Press) based on three plants (from 6000 species) found in the Botanic Gardens Glasgow: pine, Japanese banana (Musa basjoo, in Japanese, *basho*) and persimmon.

As part of Japan 2001, a year-long festival of events, six Scottish poets were invited to make a short poem on any aspect of these plants. In addition, with Yushin Toda, I made versions of traditional haiku on these plants.

The cover is a wraparound photograph of a Japanese banana leaf by Morven Gregor. The seal of office of Poet in Residence, as well as those of Yushin Toda and Morven Gregor, were stamped on some copies.

A beautiful reprint of some of the persimmon poems in a handprinted green folder on handmade paper, each poem separated by persimmon-coloured handmade paper, was subsequently published as a keepsake, at the time of the planting of the Kaki Tree. (Persimmon is *kaki* in Japanese.) The reprint, by Galdragon Press, was free of charge and given away on that occasion, at random.

## dualchas beo (1990)

taigh-fearainn teaghlach
mhaighstir inouaye
arsaidheachd dubh na shailthean
am meadhoin-bhaile lainnireach tokyo

cal is feoil is grain
air duilleag musa basjoo

cruinneachadh fhineachan
le bard mar aoidh
a seinn a dhan mu
ghilead luasganach sneachda

Aonghas MacNeacail

### a living tradition (1990)

the family farmhouse
of inouaye-san
dark antiquity in its timbers
in glittering down-town Tokyo

greens and meat and rice
on a musa basjoo leaf

a gathering of clans
whose poet-guest
declaims his song on
snow's restless whiteness

zorrozai   tincture   substitute

Matsuo Basho
translated by
Gerry Loose with
Yushin Toda

planting a basho

how hateful these

    weed seedlings

Masaoka Shiki
translated by
Gerry Loose with
Yushin Toda

    the corridor

      turns & turns

    the basho

Kobayashi Issa
translated by
Gerry Loose with
Yushin Toda

the mother eating

the sour bits

mountain persimmons

# sgial persimmon

anns an leabhar
na d'iomadachd dath
na d'iomadachd chruth
na d'dhiomhaireachd

na d'abachd
bho unnsa gu punnd
searbh gu siuchrach
cho lionmhor do sheorsa

ach air sgeilp an t-sar-mhargaidh
na do lasair cruinn orach
ceireach le milseachd

Aonghas MacNeacail

### a persimmon tale

in the book
your spectrum of colours
your kaleidoscope of shapes
your mystery

in your ripeness
from ounce to pound
from tart to honeyed
abundant variety

but on the supermarket shelf
you're a round flame of gold
waxy with sweetness

aletheia   inscapade

Valerie Gillies

hundred foot high pines

sway above her white cottage –

shallow roots below


Ian Stephen

**For Louis**

Scots Pines rampant
Barbizon and Bournemouth.

Green sways, bending
up from stony rootholds.

Salts in sap,
an Atlantic species
sniffs Pacific.


Thomas A Clark

Whenever you listen
to wind in the pines
you are not listening
to wind in the pines

## Bilingual Haiku

*ka . . . ka . . . kaki*

taste of persimmon

voice of the crow

Alan Spence

that pine I planted

getting old too

autumn winds

Kobayashi Issa
translated by
Gerry Loose
with Yushin Toda

## After Basho

Alan Spence

Learn how to pine
from the pine.

*from children:*   Christmas   blue

# Invitations Transformed

a poem

a seed
of change

midsummer matauri 2003

Paper, coloured card and postcard invitations were sent out for each event during this period. Always pushing at the boundaries of what is considered poetry, they were designed to intrigue and to make sure people remembered (and came) to the event in question.

Some contained poems, others prose; some, lists; each was pertinent to a particular event. Some were folded to reveal odd juxtapositions of words, with the meaning revealed when the invitation was fully opened.

One was folded inside a photograph; others contained (relevant) seeds or leaves.

Early this morning

falling silently, a single

paulownia leaf

Issa
translation by
Sam Hamill from the
invitation to
*live leaf / live leaf*
an installation
throughout the
Botanic Gardens by
Morven Gregor

blossom    bewitched    seagull

**blawort**
danewort
felwort
figwort

**flag**   *seleasdair*   seggan   Iris pseudacorus

gipsywort
glasswort
lousewort   hinny flooer
lungwort
milkwort
motherwort
mugwort
navelwort
nipplewort
ragwort
St John's wort
sawwort
sneezewort
soapwort
squinancywort
**stitchwort**   *tursach*
toothwort

**wordwort**

woundwort
**yellowwort**

from the invitation
to the first flying of the
Poetry Flag

ship, barque, brig, schooner, sloop, cutter, sgoth,
scow, **launch**, skiff, dinghy, wherry, cobble,punt,
catamaran, coracle, currach,  naomhog, gondola,
caravel, caique, canoe, kayak, hooker,dhow,  sampan,
galleon, ketch, smack, lugger, packet, yacht, barge,
tender, ferry,

**a marine, fleet, armada, flotilla**

the boats will take the poems along the River Kelvin
to the Clyde River, Firth of Clyde, past Arran, to the
Atlantic Ocean, amusing ducks, making fishes laugh,
sending frogs scurrying, ruffling swans' feathers,
singing to seals, waving to fisherfolk and bringing
light to the hearts of shipwrecked mariners – **the
ocean will wave its thanks**

from the invitation
(folded into a paper
boat) to the massed
launch  of the paper
boat poems by
schoolchildren

# THE KAKI TREE

August 9th, 1945, the atomic bomb blast in Nagasaki destroyed nearly all life there. Among the debris was one surviving kaki tree. (Kaki is the Japanese for persimmon). In 1993, Dr Ebinuma, an arboriculturist and a native of Nagasaki treated this ailing tree and succeeded in growing saplings from its seed, making the saplings available to Japanese children as a symbol of world peace.

In 1995 the artist Tatsuo Miyajima was deeply moved by the existence of the seedlings and started a revolutionary artistic project – Revive Time Kaki Tree Project, a planting of more of those saplings by children, with anyone who wishes to take part becoming an equal in the project.

I first became aware of the Kaki tree in 1999, through a friend then working at the Earth Centre, and corresponded with Tatsuo Miyajima, and later travelled to Japan to discuss the possibility of bringing a sapling to Glasgow.

The tree was finally planted in spring 2002 in the Botanic Gardens by children from East Park School, with assistance from the Lord Provost of Glasgow. Also present were the Consul of Japan and members of the Clydebank Life Story Group, who had all been victims of the bombing of Clydebank in that war which saw the atomic bomb dropped on Nagasaki.

The occasion was officially celebrated by peace raps from among the asylum seekers of Cleveden High School, drama students (some on stilts and with enormous costumes) from the Supported Learning

Groups at Glasgow College of Nautical Studies, pupils from local secondary and primary schools, Psycho Taiko, a Japanese drumming group, and Rising Dragon Tai-chi.

Unofficially the event was celebrated by hundreds of concerned people from all over Scotland, reading poems, telling stories, making music, photographing, making videos and quietly contemplating the tree and its meanings. The simple and poetic act of planting a tree became a symbol for all that was happening at the Botanics (and about to happen in the 'theatre of war' again).

Shortly after that planting, the Kaki tree was stolen. It never re-appeared. I like to think of it growing in a suburban garden, radiating its own kind of peace, regardless of the intentions of its new servant, the person who stole it.

Unknown to the thief, we had been given two saplings from the same seed source. One remains planted in a safe place to this day, where, in 2006, for the first time, it bore literal fruit.

One year to the day after the original planting I issued an invitation to a quiet celebration: **replanting the kaki tree**, which again was attended by throngs of people, now sobered: the country was again at war. We planted a kaki tree from another source, to stand in for the Nagasaki tree until such time as it'll be strong enough and large enough to not be uprooted and stolen, when it will then take its rightful place.

The invitation contained these words:

*A tree of course is itself and has the quickness of sentience, its own inherence and worth, not impinging on the human order of things.*

*It is also a symbol for the human world – of wildness, of economic or aesthetic importance (sometimes both at once). It also addresses something within us that we do not address for ourselves in a direct manner. It speaks eloquently, without causality, without even speech, of our relations with the non-human.*

*The kaki tree spoke to us also of our interdependence: our relations to other humans and to the non-human world; it spoke too (as a symbol) of inhumanity. It spoke of the thousands of people killed in the horror of the atom-bombing of Nagasaki, and by extension, the countless dead of other wars.*

*Thus, it is also a symbol of and for peace.*

*A tree may be cut, broken, uprooted even, and demonstrate our thoughtless regard for the non-human world; our lack of regard for fellow humans and our disrespect for the consequences of our capacity for inhumanity.*

*If a tree is uprooted it dies. It is not possible, however, to uproot a symbol. The symbolic is a product of intention. Our intention for the kaki tree was for it to stand (in our place) as a sentinel for compassionate behaviour towards each other, towards that which shares the planet with us and as a light for the possibility of peace. That intention cannot be uprooted; and in a symbolic way a new tree will stand for the original tree.*

*Nothing is ever lost; this kaki tree then, stands equally as a symbol for commemoration and for peace. As it grows, its message will spread to new generations; as long as there are new generations, as long as there is hope, as long as there is need, kaki trees will be planted here to remind us of that.*

## Persimmon

*(Nagasaki Kaki: Kibble Palace, Glasgow 2002)*

Not a sign of our reluctance to care

    of our willingness to understand

    of our refusal to love

    of our failure to utterly destroy

    but

    a symbol of resilience

    a symbol of strength

    a symbol of success

Joe Murray

A datum for all of our children

moosaknee   sweets   hope

*opposite*
on the wild stone at the
foot of the kaki tree

*& above*
the Japanese is:

*ho no o ha na*

here in calligraphy by
Hatsuo Uegaki Deputy
Mayor of Kunohe in
northern Honshu

cat   love   sun   friend

## The Poetry Flag & May Day

Since the Botanics was now flying the flag for poetry, it seemed only fitting that there should be an actual flag. Artist Pam Sandals, who specialises in flags and banners, was commissioned to make a flag that incorporated two words – on one side the flag should read **word** and on the other should read **wort**, another name for plant, still used in plant names like St John's wort.

Her brilliant design, with beautifully scripted text in blue and yellow, and measuring twelve feet by nine (3 x 4 metres) – large enough at the top of the Botanic's sixty foot flagpole to be seen from all parts - was first flown on May Day, 2000 and flew at every event after that.

The first flying was to the sound of the bagpipes and watched by scores of people who had come to celebrate the event – it helped that May Day was sunny and has long been a day of public celebration and political meaning in Glasgow.

The public had previously been invited to write their favourite word, which could be sent or hung from a tree or bush on the day. Many words came in, some beautifully embroidered, others crayoned by children. All were hung on the day, giving the whole of the Gardens a rakish air. It was like walking through an immense three-dimensional poem.

After the flag raising there was a reading in the Kibble Palace.

**Celebrate**: to publicly commemorate by ceremonies and marks of joy.

In two words – ***word wort***, the **flag** celebrates language and plants.

**Flag**, Iris pseudacorus (Gaelic seilasdair; Scots seggan, also known as yellow flag; floure-de-Loose): 'there are many kinds, some are tall and great, some little, small and low. It doth in two daies at the most take away the blewnesse' (blues) ***John Gerard 1597***
    'The yellow flag had become a poet's plant by the nineteenth century' ***Geoffrey Grigson 1958***

**Wordwort**, Verbum speciosum: a highly variable perennial. It is propagated chiefly by means of 'books', which contain its thin papery leaves. It is fertilized by the human imagination.
    A bed of wordwort is called a 'poem'.
    It has many uses, for healing, soothing, as a tonic, and in combination with other plants, such as the Songwort (Cantus mellifluous). ***Colin Will 2000***

from the invitation to
attend on May Day

# The underfunder's utopia

the state hospital
with one bed

always full
always efficient

Tom Leonard
from the reading
on May Day

*from Santiago de Compostela:*   dessimication   azafata

## Paper Boats

Since the River Kelvin flows through and alongside the Botanic Gardens, three local primary schools were invited to workshops to make poems about water. The results were written on squares of paper and folded into paper boats.

They were joined by a fourth school in a mass launching of the paper boats from the riverbank, where the boats bobbed their course to join the Clyde and the open sea.

Water, water. Let me think, let me think a
bathroom stream. Splish Splash Splosh
Drip drap drop. The steam goes
to the clouds then it starts to rain

Swaleyha Jahengar
Willowbank Primary School
for a paper boat

Sometimes I wish I could be a fish
and my tail would swish

I would jump up and down
and sometimes I would frown

Sometimes I would hear fish whoosh
ing past, I would say shoosh

Splish splash I am having a bath I
don't know what for I never get dirty

I am going to bed swim swim swish
swish splosh whoosh woosh goodnight

Cristo    refuxio    rattata

Kayleigh Hanley
Hill's Trust Primary
for a paper boat

## Water Wonderland

The mermaids sit in the blue lagoon
Splish splashing their wet scaly tails
The dolphins sing a sweet melody
Making swish swash as they & the
Whales swim through the water
Water fall whooshing while I'm
Wondering where water goes
It goes to the sky
To the great god Neptune
With his beautiful daughter Neptuna
Whose friends are the Selkies
The seal people.
Children play in the bay
With Starfish, Angelfish &
Seahorses paddling in the shallow water
There we will leave them &
Their friends in a
Water wonderland

Roisín Robinson
Hillhead Primary
for a paper boat

# Launches and Readings

Like any gardener, when conditions were right, I branched out; I borrowed (like 'borrowing' cuttings with your secateurs from someone else's garden).

I invited many poets to launch a book at the Kibble Palace; sometimes also visiting poets from overseas were invited, as were those taking part in some wider festival. Thus with a very small budget, but by piggyback riding on publishers and festival organisers I was able to present many poets and their work.

Some events were devised by me in association with other organisations for special occasions, like World Book Day or National Poetry Day (though at the Botanic Gardens that was every day).

All the readings took place in The Kibble Palace, to a resident audience of exotic plants as well as invited guests. Many were closed evening events, some were at lunchtime with strolling parents and toddlers, office workers hoping for a quiet sandwich, gardeners come to borrow. The evening readings were frequently interrupted by the sound of sirens from nearby streets; now and then an owl would hoot or a sparrow rush round the dome; the atmospheric dripping of rain from glass onto heads and books; the gloom induced by downpours and storms - but the poets' words soon dispelled the outside world – for a moment we had a palace of poetry and plants, despite the cold of winter and the heat of summer.

Wine was sometimes drunk on these occasions and music always, from Bach to traditional fiddle, pipes and song, jazz saxophone and oud and drums and keyboard.

### Reading at the Kibble Palace, Glasgow
*for Richard Price*

The poet kibbled among flowers: acanthus and lilac,
the extremely unglaswegian hosted beneath our palace
of glass, twined to our iron buttresses and trellises.
Under the dripping threshold of Botanic Gardens our
poet launched his poems at us as we parked our bums
in the very entrance-way to Eden. And then his quiet
voice gathered them, infallibly, gathered the people
to the previously quiet lychgate to the flowers; as if he
had unlocked the trees, unbraided the long ears of the
palms and now folk could walk past, past the poet's
words and use them to step in, lie or sit on benches and
eat their noisy lunch-box apples.Pigeons shuffled the
rainy roof above his head, dealing his words to the air,
to the children's cries which took them up and trumped
them with their own. And all the people passed him,
indifferent, embarrassed, apologetic, smiling, stony-
faced, indignant, but each pocketed, each snuck up a
word as he side-stepped them in mid-flight: 'trout are
influential', 'aquaflora', of course, caught like burrs on
the double buggy's wheels as it carriaged weans towards
the greenery. 'A hem of air' stitched a down-and-out's
frayed hems and the name 'Fiona' savoured the lips of
a royally built black woman who tossed it back to you
with nonchalant contempt. And they were there, the
people, not listening to you but listening as their bodies
took the imprint of that awkwardness where language
washed like a sea taken from its element and dashed
about the Kibble's deck. And later they'll remember the
day they dodged your words to make their rendezvous
with plants, faced down poems to make their tryst with
fronds. Not that they'll thank you but they'll think about
language and it will thank them for you.

David Kinloch

## Landscape with Signs

A woman driving on a straight road into a country
at the threshold of memory    looks forward
through a windscreen glazed with dust
into a sun-crossed tunnel of fruit trees
The picture glitters with the metal rim of a door
thrown open    trajectories of vision crashing
into the camera lens off the muddied white Toyota
The car has no wing mirrors    each surface
is an image    the sky is specular with wings
She has paused in front of a sign spelt
Splendour    Red Delicious    Ice-cream pear
Snow melts from the hill slopes    hot sunlight
over the apple stores    the small square houses
of Ettrick    The road runs ahead of her
into the fruitlands    each sweet spring
sugar-candied    breaks into a basket of angles
Soon she'll be through the blossom's bridal promise
of loveliness on crabbed branches    into a country
she doesn't yet recognise    a heartland
both harsh and tender    cramped and open    arid
and burgeoning    is her own    is what her life is
the dry blue ridges    the deep fast river
which makes fertile the orchards
where in this season of her life she finds herself

Gerrie Fellows
from the launch of
*The Duntroon Toponymy*
(Mariscat, 2001)

queimada    chocolate    caballero

'Fly, poem …'


Fly, poem, say, poem
to each and every human being
we are indeed alive, there's hope –
there's time, its ear is there for tweaking.

Calm the quaking little soul
of the rich – mercy is in the wings.
Love and liberty don't show
tumblers of blood, but living springs.

Tell the hardest-working poor
with a calf-mouth, pendant, thoughtful –
gnaw into their hearts – no need for
heroes if that should be impossible.

('*Szàllj költemény …*')

Attila József
translated by Edwin Morgan
from the launch of
*Attila József, Sixty Poems*
(Mariscat, 2001)


zopilote    nascimento

## Hunang og blóð

Til eru skáld
sem vakna andfúl að morgni
fá sér harðsoðið egg með blaðinu
hunang í teið
en frussa svo í vaskinn:
Oj blóðbragð
Önnur vakna
í tungumálið
teygja sig blíðgrimm
í elsku sína og vekja
henni blóð:
Mmm hunang


### Honey an blöd

Der's poets
at waaken wi a waageng i da
moarnin
hae a herd-boiled egg wi da paper
honey i der tae
but dan sproot i da basin:
Gadge! Da taste o blöd
Idders waaken
inta tongues
rekk oot, currie-coorse
tae da loved wan an tize
her blöd
Mmm honey

## Mêl a Gwaed

Mae 'na feirdd
sy'n deffro gyda cheg fel cesail camel
a gyda'u wy 'di berwi a'r papur bore
yn cymryd mêl yn eu te
cyn poeri I'r basn
- ychafi! Blas gwaed.
Mae eraill yn deffro
i fyd llawn tafodau
gan ymestyn yn dyner, ddidostur
tua'u cariadon, a'u deffro
trwy dynnu gwaed:
mmm, blas mêl.

Thorarinn Eldjárn
translated into
Shetlandic by
Christine De Luca
& Welsh by
Elin ap Hywel
as part of
*Nordic-Celtic Connections*

*more from Scotland:*    plumptious    perpetual

**Bàs**

Tha Gàidhlig a' dol bàs.
Seadh.

Well, 's e tha mi 'g ràdh
Gu bheil i dol às –
Mar gun canadh tu – gu math clever.

See, eil thu tuigsinn,
Chan eil vocabulary
No het mar sin aice
A tha freagarrach ceart
Dhan t-saoghal againn
'S chan urrainn dhi cumail suas
Ris na bigwigs.

Aidh. Shin agad e.
That's it –
End of story.
Gaylick's fucked, so it is. Fucked forever.

**Language Death**

The Gaylick is dying.
Seadh.

Well, what I mean is:
she's going from it –
as you might say – gu math clever.

Seadh, eil thu tuigsinn
we don't have the vocabulary
or rud sam bith mar sin
that's suitable
for the saoghal-mòr today
and she can't keep up
with the balaich mhòra.

Aye. Shin agad e.
That's it –
cnag na cùise.
The Gaylick's fucked, tha –
Fucked gu siorraidh.

Rody Gorman
from the launch of
*On The Underground
Air A' Charbad Fo Thalamh*
(Polygon, 2000)

lemon    bum    salient

## Botanics Man

He's snipping spent marguerites
with October secateurs
when this moth
rises from the roots.

End-of-season brown
he prunes it too,
snips and snaps it
to a moth with bobbled wings

which bounces
till he toes
a wellyload of soil
on its soft impertinence.

Valerie Thornton
from the launch of
*Catacoustics*
(Mariscat, 2000)

WANDERING ONTO A BEACH at low tide, he starts to
walk, seeing only an edge of scalloped sand extending
into the distance, without shadow or interruption,
under the diffused light of a  winter sky. He feels no
hunger or cold and it is as if he could go on like this
for ever, into a distance always further, and he thinks
of nothing

except the most intolerable of paradoxes: to dread
everything closing in when it is the emptiness of the
world which baffles.

Gael Turnbull
from the launch of
*MIGHT A SHAPE OF WORDS*
*and other transmutations*
(Mariscat, 2000)

flittermouse   gleam   sunflower

## Unappreciated Therapy

Is that Jake from Finnieston on the line

*Aye     that's right Erchie*
*an afore I raise ma point*
*ah'd jist like tae say     yir show's pure spot on by the way*

Well     *ta much* Jake     I'm glad you like it

*Listen Erchie     whit ah want tae talk aboot*
*is the guy who wis oan earlier*
*asking if he should play the piana*
*cause it soothed his nerves*

That's right Jake
I'm a firm believer in someone
developing their musical talents
especially if it helps relieve them
of the stress of life in the fast lane so to speak

*Well     ah stey up above him*
*in the slow lane so tae speak*
*an ah canny get tae sleep*
*in fact   the whole hoose canny get tae sleep*
*in fact   the whole sterrheid canny get tae sleep*
*whit wi Liberace doonsterrs giein it mince oan the ivories*

*so ah'd jist like tae say wan thing Erchie*

*thanks a bunch*
*          thanks a fuckin bunch*

mirth    badger    wendy

Brian Whittingham
from the launch of
*The Old Man from Brooklyn
& the Charing Cross Carpet*
(Mariscat, 2000)

## Song for the Song of the White-Throated Sparrow

Before it can stop itself, the mind
has leapt up inferences, crag to crag,
the obvious arpeggio. Where there is a doorbell
there must be a door – a door
meant to be opened from inside.
Door means house means – wait a second –
but already it is standing on a threshold previously
known to be thin air, gawking. The Black Spruce
points to it: clarity,
melting into ordinary morning, true
north. Where the sky is just a name,
a way to pitch a little tent in space and sleep
for five unnumbered seconds.

Don McKay
at the event
*Two Canadian Poets*

A good laugh aids digestion. Add
the practical necessity of freedom

and you get a knock-down argument
for telling after-dinner jokes. Yet

the soul, like noumena,
unknowable –

out past the last outpost of reason
*We yet* comprehend *it is*

*incomprehensible.* Open the door.
Sunlight and singing. *All that we may ask.*

Jan Zwicky
from the sequence
'Kant and Bruckner:
Twelve Variations'
at the event
*Two Canadian Poets*

bastard   star   boots

### In the Kibble Palace

In the Kibble Palace with its dazzling statues
And glass dome, reading a poet I've just come across,
I learn that under ice the killer whale

Seeing anything darker than snow, falls away
Then charges, smashing the ice with his forehead,
Isolating seal or man on a drifting piece

Of the floe. Imagine those tons of blubber
Thrusting up; tail curvetting
As the hammer head hits. What if the skull

Should split, splinters penetrate to the brain?
Nor will dry land protect us from the thudding
In the blood, those forces below. How can we conquer

Stewart Conn
celebrating National
Poetry Day 1999

Who cannot conquer ourselves? I shall think of this
When, fishing on frosted glass, I find
My line tightening against the swell;

Or hearing you moan and turn in your sleep
I know you are on your own, far out,
Dark shapes coursing below. Meanwhile

The horizon closes in, a glass
Globe. We will admit it is there
When it is too late; and blunder for the exits

To find them locked. Seeing as though through ice
Blurred forms gyrate, we will put our heads
Together and try to batter a way out.

## walking in the park

am I a spectator at
your sport with yourself

or are we together, as one
sharing the day, under a common sun;

is this a day
in our shared life and time

or you, seen through the hole in the air
that lets my eyes consider you, walking there

beside me . when this is all done
who is to say

what happened this day, whether
sensing your beauty

Tom Leonard
celebrating National
Poetry Day 1999

was just / the echo of nothing
to do with me or the inside of me

but you and your private sense of being
on this another such occasion

ecru   onomatopoeia

### The Beekeeper
*for Carol Ann Duffy*


Happy as haystacks are my quiet hives
from this distance and
through the bevel of this window's glass.
This is the place I robe myself
in net and hat and gloves.
This is my vestibule,
crocked like a dairy, full
of the sexual smell of bees.

Bees that fizzle out singly
like smoke rising from one cigarette
then straighten-up and fly right
hauled
by olfactory magnets
while, loaded, laden,
their fellow workers make a beeline home.

This is the business,
and I mind the time the old man,
showing me my first stuffed queen, the
tawny intricate purpose moving on the quiet comb,
made me initiate of this gold, this goodness.
He taught me the riddle of Samson –
*Out of the strong came forth sweetness –*
the honeycomb in the lion's carcase.

*Out of the eater comes something to eat*

*Out of the strong comes something sweet.*

I flip my net back
and go bare-armed on and out to them
wishing only to trust my own good husbandry
and do nothing
nothing but feel them
crawl and trawl the follicles, stamens
and pistils of my unpollened arms.

Liz Lochhead
who read at the
Valentine Tree 2001
event

*from Guadalupe River:*   rudder   love   knuckle

لن تقتلوني

أموتُ على طريقتي
وأحفر قبري بأيديّاني

أخيطُ كفني بروحتي
وأرسمُ عليهِ صورة
لجلادي

أعمدُ نفسي بدموع
لقهر وأودعُ بالشهود
طيَّ إنسان

أمنحُ تركتي من غير ظلم،
وأهدي للحُر حصاني

بأحملُ نفسي وأرتدي
سوادَ الليل
وأرتلُ صورَ قرآني

وأمشي في جنازتي
ويساعدني قلبي وأحساسي
وريدي وشرياني

وأكتبُ وصيتي على شهد
قبري بدمي
للقدسِ قصائدا
وأغاني

سأبكي على نفسي .. فرحا
بالموت
وأهدي للظالم كل أحزاني

Ghazi Hussein
translated by
Saad Ibrahim
at the
*WORD OF THE WORLD*
event for & by asylum
seekers & refugees
in association with
Scottish PEN as part of
First Nights festival

You Will Not Kill Me

I will die on my own terms
And I will dig my grave with my bare hands
And stitch together my shroud with my own hair
And draw on it the murderer's picture,
And anoint my self with the tears of oppression
And bid farewell with yearning for every human being.
And bequeath my penury without favour
Leaving my horse to the free.
I will carry my coffin
And wear the darkness of night
And recite verses from the Quraan.
And walk in my own cortege
And the bearers will be my heart and senses,
My veins and arteries.
Write my epitaph on my tombstone with my blood
- poems and songs dedicated to Jerusalem.
I will mourn my own self
Rejoicing in death
Heaping all my lamentations on the unjust.

No earth.
No shroud.
No rites
Blessed are the vultures on a clearing mission
Praise marauding worms interning each item
Baby,
Papa,
Mama,
Nana,
Baba.
Sheep
Goat
Hen
Cat
Dog
Kitten
And all
that

'a generation expedited in a whiff to their forefathers',
reads the epitaph.

Amadu Khan
accompanying himself
on drum at the
WORD OF THE WORLD
event for & by asylum
seekers & refugees
in association with
Scottish PEN as part of
First Nights festival

from very young children:    hug    art

Imagine great monotonous stretches of uncharted, unnamed territory, imagine vast eroded plateau and postglacial beaches. The time is the end of the Boreal period, the beginning of the archaic times called 'Atlantic'. Sudden mists, strange lights and lightnings, and up there, far above, moon, sun, stars: appearances, disappearances, constellations. The earthscape is mineral, dominated by great stone blocks fallen from obscure disasters, and by scatterings of fragmented rock. In such a context, geometry (a point, a line, a circle) can be a kind of salvation, especially if you can feel that you're establishing a correspondence with what you haven't yet got around to calling a cosmos.

It's a world of primitive geometry and primal meteorology.

Later on, the stories come in. Some of these stories (you hear of petrified armies, of druid sacrifices, all kinds of spookiness and collective unconscious hookery-pookery) are more attractive than others. I like the Hebridean one that tells of craggy rocks arriving by boat on Lewis accompanied by folk (they sound like shamans) dressed in feathers ... All this is what some people call 'poetry'. But the real poetics are elsewhere: in the open space, in the migratory movement, the elemental necessity, the primal gesture. You can go further by trying to read beyond the legends. Beginning with the grainy touch of the stone itself, and its lichens.

As to the theories, the interpretations and the calculations, I listen to them attentively, in a stony silence, before moving back to some rock, any old rock on shore or moor on which frost and sea-salt have written the weather of the ages.

Kenneth White
from the talk & reading:
*Living on the Earth*
(also the Botanic
Gardens launch of
*House of Tides*)

## Poacher's Poem

Is soilleir cù dubh air liana bhàin
Is soilleir cù ban air liana dhuibh,
Na'm bithinn ri fiadhach nam beann
Be'n cù riabhach mo roghainn.

A snowy field shows up the sable hound
The white dog's seen on dusky ground
The brindle hound will be my choice
To hunt in the moorland's own disguise.

Valerie Gillies
from a reading in
association with the
Poetry Association of
Scotland (& where she
imitated an owl so
perfectly the small birds
in the Kibble Palace
darted for cover)

love    happy    football

## Moving On

Square pegs in round holes
yet ready for what life unfolds
we know what the future holds
for the Gypsies
it is the gift for the precious few
but the Gypsies know
Move on, that's what the Gypsies will do.

Laughter will shatter the ruins of the world
you'll hear it from the Gypsies
and music will prevail,
when the caged birds are silenced
music from the Gypsies
Mothers singing beyond walls and over waters
the voice of the Gypsies
And the young will renew the old
as memories are retold, retold
for what is time to all of we
for we are every Romany

Move on again, Yes that's what we do
and we will find a tale or two
The old world is our breath, our heart

and our start, is where we finish
forever, moving on.

Mally Dow
from
*Poetry and Storytelling*
an event as part of
*Open Roads 2000*
*International Romany &*
*Travellers Festival*

bowling   everyone   mummy   daddy

## Absinthe with Eddie

There's an age that people get stuck at.
(Some of my schoolfriends were already forty,
and still are; others hit adolescence once,
and never moved on.)

*You're* different. You're younger than when we first met
a generation ago. While the rest of us have been taking
                    good hold
of the passing years, turning them into something solid
and durable around us – to keep the world out
and ourselves trapped safely in – you've been
                    dismantling Time
and Space into words, sounds and silences ...

Some friends and I paid you a visit recently.
Lunch over, you prepared an afternoon tray of glasses
and illegal absinthe. You invited us
to *go on*, to *give it a try* –

When I picture you now I picture you smiling:
in every poem, you're offering us the unexpected taste
of Life itself – as something altogether new
and ours for the having

Ron Butlin
at the launch of
*Unknown is Best A*
*celebration of Edwin*
*Morgan at eighty* a
surprise book on
the occasion of his
birthday party in the
Kibble Palace

# At Eighty

Push the boat out, compañeros,
Push the boat out, whatever the sea.
Who says we cannot guide ourselves
through the boiling reefs, black as they are,
the enemy of us all makes sure of it!
Mariners, keep good watch always
for that last passage of blue water
we have heard of and long to reach
(no matter if we cannot, no matter)
in our eighty-year-old timbers
leaky and patched as they are but sweet,
well seasoned with the scent of woods
long perished, serviceable still
in unarrested pungency
of salt and blistering sunlight. Out,
push it all out into the unknown!
Unknown is best, it beckons best,
like distant ships in mist, or bells,
clanging ruthless from stormy buoys.

Edwin Morgan
Poet Laureate of
Scotland on his
eightieth birthday party
at the Botanic Gardens

*from one person with a lot of favourite words:*   porcupine   bid-dup

# EXHIBITIONS & INSTALLATIONS

Poetry is notoriously difficult to define, and my intention had always been to highlight the diversity of poets' work (complementing the plants' own diversity at the Botanics): monoculture is stifling.

In order to use the whole of the Botanics – Curators and the Manager had set no limits on what could happen – it seemed logical to include exhibitions of the work of poets in other media. Some of our poets were also photographers, others had sculptural aspects to their work, yet others had no words, but shed new light with their captivating silence.

Accordingly, there were manifestations everywhere, some more conventional exhibitions, others scattered about the Gardens waiting to be discovered by passers-by.

**hear singing?**

**no**
**must be the heat**
**the humidity**

**the veil of flies**
**before your face**

The wildlife of the Glasgow Botanics
now includes
an infestation of small songs

Optimum conditions 28 centigrade / humidity: 100%

small songs catch the light
check for tell-tale brightness amongst orchids
epiphytes
fruit-bearing trees

and for glinting in sphagnum

bromeliads, which shelter small amphibians,
may also prove attractive to voices seeking hosts

from the flier for
*Rogue Seeds*
an exhibition by
Jen Hadfield
of 'small songs':
poems printed on
acetate & hung
throughout the main
range of glasshouses
& elsewhere

shantih    spelunking    quicksilver

ε

double wedding –

white apple's blossom

fugue passage
of Spring


ζ

stars in pairs

John Hudson
from starWoodSTONE
a poetry installation
on the big lawn & above
in the form of the
constellation Lyra

lovers in the long grass
rolling

on the reed-dark earth

MY WATERS ALWAYS KNOW THEIR COURSE TO RIVERMOUTH FROM HILLTOP SOURCE MANS DESTINATION IS UNKENT UNTIL HIS JOURNEY IS FULL SPENT

Liz Niven
from Cree Lines poems
for the
Cree River Walk
an exhibition
in the Kibble Palace

swaddle     totem

彼采葛兮
一日不見
如三月兮

彼采蕭兮
一日不見
如三秋兮

彼采艾兮
一日不見
如三歲兮

poem-proclamation
from one of many
on the Garden's
noticeboards & poems
seen & heard elsewhere
in the Gardens
reflecting the many
mother tongues
in Scotland

## Dances & Tales

Storytelling is another aspect of poetry. Oral traditions still heard in Scotland today were the original means of transmission for poetry, the accessible written word being a relative newcomer. Storytellers seldom made the same distinctions that we do today, between poetry, saga, history, genealogy, praise, epic & so on. They just told it, usually to music and often as part of a theatrical or religious performance of which it was an integral part.

Ewan McVicar & Gift-Amu Logotse on different occasions both wove stories from the inspiration of the Kibble Palace hothouse as part of *In the Rainforest*.

The drama to this day remains compelling. On one occasion outside on a bitter February morning, dance-performers were cold & also painted blue; one spectator was found phoning for an ambulance – she feared the dancers were frostbitten.

For thirteen days now he had been eating only roses. On the south-facing wall of the cottage was a climbing rose, older certainly than himself and still in bloom despite frost despite wind despite the lack of love. Each morning he stepped from the house in stockinged feet, trousers almost on, bare bodied, bare headed, and sniffed at every bud. The rose was as ill-kempt as he and scrambled rather than rambled around the gutters and onto the roof. Smelling every flower meant balancing on a broken step-ladder and climbing the lower reaches of the roof, slates and knees cracking. After the first sniff the bud would either be passed over or cut with a small pair of nail scissors and shoved in his pocket. Each morning ten flowers were collected, chosen for their fragrance and taken back into the house along with many scratches from the thorns, which were ancient and long.

Alex Rigg
from *Roses*
in the free booklet
*Jigg of Slurrs*
stories accompanying a
performance event
*In No Mind*

## In stone

While most of the work was seasonal, with a brief flowering appearance, there was some work with a more perennial aspect.

Although keen not to litter the Gardens with inscribed poems, three locations demanded attention – the Kaki Tree, the Poetry Garden and the centenary of the 'B' listed Kirklee Bridge, a massive Victorian structure straddling the river Kelvin where it runs through the Botanic Gardens. This commission was delayed by the need for planning permission from Historic Scotland and Glasgow City Council (who did all they could to help).

The poems in the Poetry Garden and on Kirklee Bridge were not intended as paper poems and should be read in their locations.

Our ref H&D/RS/EM
Your ref
Date 15 November 2000

**PROPOSED ENGRAVING OF POETRY ON THE
BASE OF PILLARS TO KIRKLEE BRIDGE – A 'B'
LISTED BUILDING WITHIN THE GLASGOW WEST
CONSERVATION AREA.**

I refer to our meeting on site of Monday 13 November
2000 to discuss the proposal to engrave lettering
forming poetry on the above property.

I can confirm that, having discussed the matter with
the Planning Officer from Development Control,
North West, Protective services, an application for
planning permission will not be required in this
instance as the works can be deemed '*de minimis*'.

However, as also discussed on site, an application for
listed building consent is required in this case since
the engraving of poetry into the original stonework
plinth on the base of the columns is considered to
constitute a consent matter.

I enclose a set of the relevant forms for your use.

Our ref: INVALID 00/03654/DC
3 January 2001


SITE:      Site at Kirklee Bridge

PROPOSAL: Formation of lettering on stonework
          plinths on base of columns supporting
          bridge.


          Your application, 00/03654/DC, was
          received on 14 December 2000, was
          incomplete and is invalid.

ADDITIONAL INFORMATION REQUIRED FOR
APPLICATION 00/03654/DC

Your application is invalid.

    01    The following plans are requested:

          3 *additional copies* of photographs
          submitted.

    02    Please define the application site with a
          red line on a plan not less than 1 : 1250
          scale. *4 copies* of plan required.

Our ref: DECISION
GCC Application ref: 00/3654/DC
Date 9 April 2001

**SITE:**      **Site at Kirklee Bridge**

**PROPOSAL:**  **Formation of lettering on stonework plinths on base of columns supporting bridge..**

I am pleased to inform you that Glasgow City Council has now taken a decision to approve your application 00/3654/DC.

**The decision notice is a legal document and should be retained for future reference.**

Jonathan Kemp, sculptor
carving text

# THE POETRY GARDEN

Designed for a quiet and under-used part of the Botanic Gardens, in front of the old Curator's house, the Poetry Garden is a place for the silence that's at the heart of poetry.

The Poetry Garden also celebrates links between Japan & Scotland (it was made during the Festival year Japan 2001) and incorporates features and notions common to both cultures. It welcomes visitors to be both active in making poetry and in sitting quietly - a place of reflection but not solemnity.

The design itself incorporates the Japanese feeling for old things re-used – *mitate* – which is also the old thrift here, & the new recycling in both countries.

The stones in the garden came from within the Botanic Gardens and are arranged as islands in a sea of moss and grass. This arranging of stones is very Japanese and also to be found in Scottish gardens and public green spaces as well as occurring naturally in both countries.

The path is of recycled slate hothouse benches, with a poem inscribed in separate lines out of sight of each other, but which can be read to make poetic sense from whichever direction it's met.

There is also a platform – the focus for readings and events – of Douglas fir felled elsewhere in the city, left untreated to weather gracefully, with a canopy of poles of giant-bamboo prunings from the Palm House.

It was adapted from a design by David Connearn for a renga platform, itself an idea of Alec Finlay, and built by Gordon Joss. Renga is an ancient Japanese form of shared poetry-making.

Planting is minimal, with only two species of fern (Polypodium vulgare and Matteucia struthioptera – one itself being recycled from the Curator's chimney breast) as well as the moss and close-cropped grass – an echo of the wider Scottish country beyond the confines of the Garden.

The garden was opened by the Consul for Japan, Mr Hiroshi Ota and a reading followed on the platform.

## The Wren

*for V.*

>        This will be your last life here. I see a dropsy
> helicopter, choring along. A heron like a sickle reaps an
> Iron-Age sun. I see the Caravan. You've been travelling
> on your own but – Dear God - like falling face down
> into warm mud, this is love – the sudden, muddy sun.

>        You have the polytunnel. Something about you
> will need protecting. A bust creel's a debt. You have a
> debt...doesn't everyone? Money is a pile of anything.
> Cabages mean money as manure does. Cool leaves creak
> between your palms in the evening. It's enough. Pull
> one.

>        I see the Wren. Behind and before, above and
> below you. That's luck And under the sun, the Dark-
> Haired Hammerer. In the gleaming grass, the ducks
> will gleam like curling stones. You'll get off scot-free,
> trusting everyone.

>        You will love the land. You will love the land
> like a bairn. The Hammerer. The Wren. The dropsy
> helicopter choring Along. The heron like a sickle reaps
> an Iron-Age sun.

Jen Hadfield

# Cabbage

I ask the garden to bear me witness –
but what the ground offers me as evening comes
looks most of all like a snoozing face –
whorled, shut, deaf to disgrace –
a mute Om from a drill of Oms
cool and creaking – a Northern lotus.

Jen Hadfield
from
*Nigh – No – Place*
Jen Hadfield
read at the opening of
the Poetry Garden

## Sing

*(homage to Gertrude Stein)*

every single thing sings
everything sings
is singular
sings
in singularity sings and rings
tell the bell
the song sung true
sing everything
is a thing is a thing
is a thing is a thing
is a thing is a thing
sing

Alan Spence
for
*wind flowers bell flowers &*
*Kyoto Poems*
National Poetry Day in
the Poetry Garden

Shoha
version by
Gerry Loose
for
*wind flowers bell flowers*

at dusk

the fountain's raceme

glistening

Onitsura
version by
Gerry Loose
for
*wind flowers bell flowers*

autumn wind

still alive and seeing ourselves

you and me

this morning's spring breeze

a shop selling kites

just opened

Ichiro Takagi
translated by
Gerry Loose & Yushin
Toda one of four
seasonal poems (this
one is summer) sent
from Kyoto Botanic
Gardens for *Kyoto Poems*

far off bell-sound

moving along coming

through spring haze

Shiki
version by
Gerry Loose
for *wind flowers bell flowers*
(in which pennants with
poems about wind were
planted on bamboo poles
throughout the Poetry
Garden and poems were
attached to the tongues
of bells hung on poles
causing the bells to ring
in the wind) for National
Poetry Day

## Films

Four short films were made during this period: **Botanics** by Donna Campbell, **The Valentine Tree** – a Millenium Postcard by Iñigo Garrido, **The Kaki Tree Project**, also by Iñigo Garrido and **Unearthed** by Vicki Fleck in which Botanic Gardens curators and gardeners read their favourite poems. Botanics, The Valentine Tree and Unearthed were shown on National Poetry Day in the Botanic Gardens, The Kaki Tree Project had a screening in Grosvenor Cinema, nearby.

## All you who sleep tonight

All you who sleep tonight
Far from the ones you love,
No hand to left or right
And emptiness above –

Know that you aren't alone
The whole world shares your tears,
Some for two nights or one
And some for all their years.

Vikram Seth
chosen by
Martin O'Loughlin
Gardener at Glasgow
Botanics for the film
*Unearthed* by Vicki Fleck

## A Glass of Water

Here is a glass of water from my well.
It tastes of rock and root and earth and rain
It is the best I have, my only spell,
And it is cold, and better than champagne.
Perhaps someone will pass this house one day
To drink, and be restored, and go his way,
Someone in dark confusion as I was
When I drank cold water in a glass,
Drank a transparent health to keep me sane
After the bitter mood had gone again.

May Sarton
chosen by
David Menzies
Curator at Glasgow
Botanics for the film
*Unearthed* by Vicki Fleck

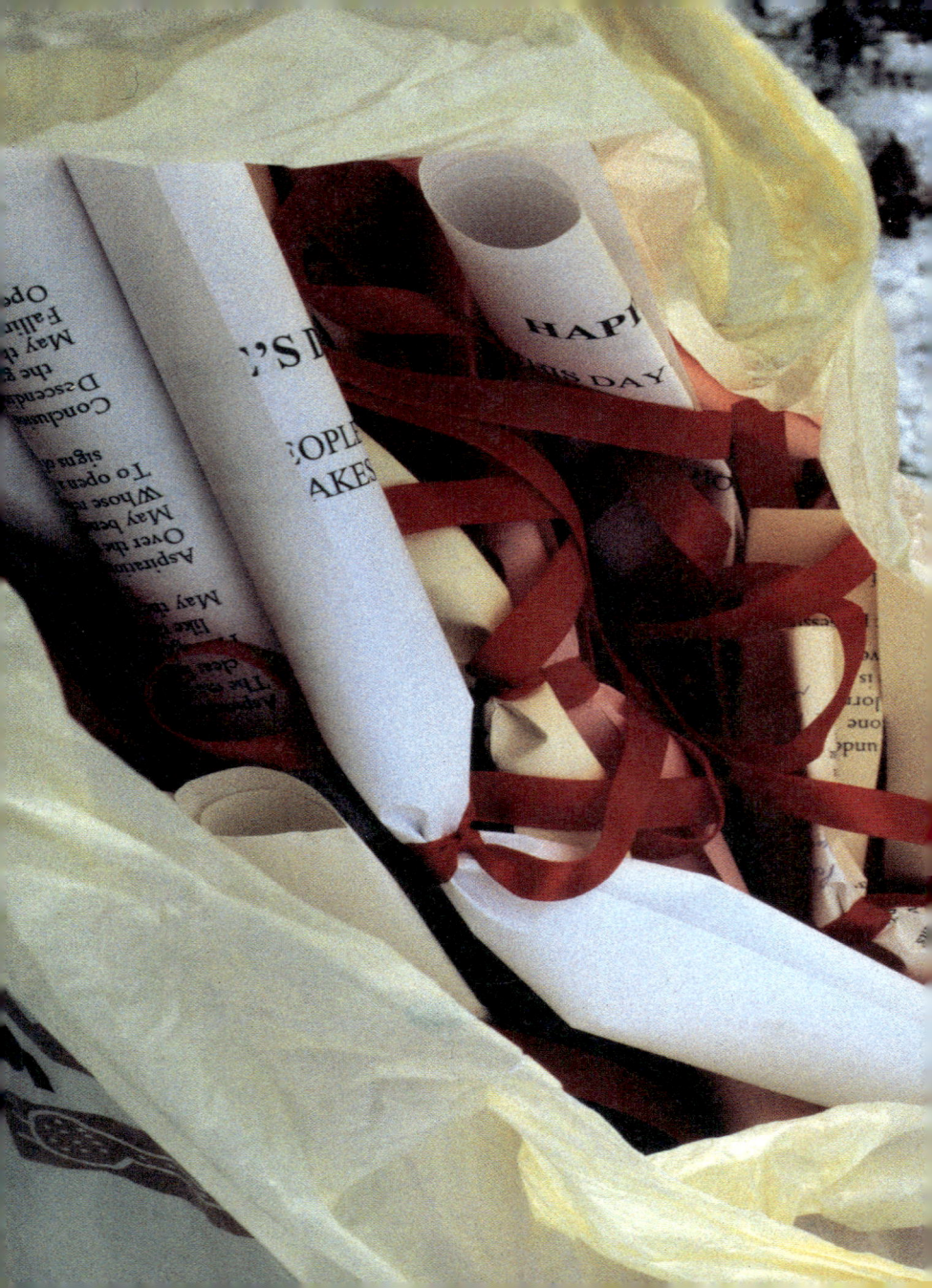